Negative Turns

By

Euneata Payne, MA

ISBN: 978-1-5882-0579-7 (sc)
ISBN: 978-1-5882-0582-7 (hc)
ISBN: 978-1-5882-0578-0 (e)

Print information available on the last page.

This book is printed on acid free paper

2021 Revised Edition

1stBooks - rev. 01/08/2021

Acknowledgements

I must first thank my parents, who brought me into the world, had it not been for them, I would not exist to write this book.

Special gratitude and appreciation to my friends and colleagues Robert Lawson, Cheryl Bennett, Kathy Lamancusa, Richard Haid, Floyd Shepherd, Stuart Atkins, Bette Williams and Justine Clark-Lomax for being there for me, I will be forever grateful.

Thank you Dennis Campbell and everyone at 1st Books who believed in me and helped in the completion and promotion of this book.

Sincere thanks to my entire family, personal friends, and business colleagues who have been a solid support system. Without them, I would not be where I am today.

A huge thank you to my partner in life, Evis Lee Payne for your love and support. Thank you from the bottom of my heart for listening and putting up with me to the end.

Special acknowledgement to Patricia Schlamadinger and Dan Poynter for your guidance and wise counsel. I thank all those who contributed to the publishing, design, layout, editing and promotion of this book; *I sincerely thank you all.*

In memory of my loving grandmother who taught me love, warmth, grace, charm, sensitivity, and **how to take out the garbage with style**

Contents

What others are saying about NEGATIVE TURNS

"Negative Turns is a must read book that will provide you with tips and strategies to help you overcome the difficulties in your life. This book will uplift your spirits again and again."

> Robert Lawson, Ed.D.
> Author

"Negative experiences are a given for the business owner. Learning how to use them to achieve excellence and success is the purpose of Negative Turns."

> Cheryl I. Bennett
> Chief, MED
> **U.S. Small Business Administration**

"Negative Turns will inspire and motivate you to eliminate the road blocks in your life. While we all experience them, Euneata has found ways to help us understand where they come from and how to move them out, leaving more energy and space in our lives for us to pursue our passions and make a difference in this world. You won't be sorry you made an investment in yourself through the principles Euneata shares in Negative Turns."

> Kathy Lamancusa
> Best-selling author of, Flowers are Forever
> International Trend Strategist

"Negative barriers hold back many people, but not Euneata and her clients. Based on Euneata's personal experiences and her more than 20 years' experience in the training field, this book will help you overcome your negative barriers as you develop action plans and communication skills to turn each component of your life around and to reach your full potential."

Richard L. Haid, Ph.D., PCC, Adult Mentor

"Immensely wise and hopeful. Negative Turns is a powerful guide for anyone seeking to overcome negative challenges in personal or business situations. Euneata Payne explains clearly and artfully the vital linkages among our attitudes, interpersonal skills and successful problem solving."

Floyd Shepherd, Ph.D., MBA

"Euneata provides the reader with inspirational stories. Then she encourages them to follow it up with practical action plans for long-term success."

Stuart Atkins, Ph.D.
President
Stuart Atkins, Inc.

"Negative Turns is positively inspirational. This book will give you personal ways to succeed and to adapt your autonomy to many situations."

Bette Williams
Discipline Dean/Counselor
Los Angeles Unified School District

"The book Negative Turns, by author Euneata Payne is truly an inspirational work of art. Negative Turns is robust in the area of self imagery. Euneata combines her personal, educational and professional experiences to capture and uniquely summarize how negativity impedes one's progress. The concepts while easy to understand, provides depth and encouragement to those who have not yet experienced the abundant life because of negative forces. The manner in which Mrs. Payne portrays herself in the book, suggests that Negative Turns is for people from all walks of life."

Justine Clark-Lomax, BS. MSW

Introduction

The first thing I will say to you is that I *don't have* "10 Points" to give you on how to manage negative influences in your life. I do not own catchy phrases. I don't have decorated words to impart.

What I *do have* is profound understanding, a "giving spirit," and a desire to share with those who have a "listening heart."

As long as I can remember, I dreamed of having a successful future, and I was determined that my life would be meaningful and extraordinary. I dreamed about it many nights. I did not have the slightest idea of how it would happen or exactly what my future might hold.

I was a plain girl from a small town called "Beltzhoover" in Pittsburgh, Pennsylvania. Pittsburgh was a great place to grow up, and I've heard it said that if you are from Pittsburgh, you are considered the salt of the earth. This meant that you were solid as a rock, hard-working, dependable with strong family values, and that was a good thing. So, I was proud to be from Pittsburgh or "The Burg" as we sometimes referred to it. However, I had meager opportunities, little influence, and few notable contacts.

I was raised in a strict, organized religious sect. As far as I was concerned, there were far too many rules and unrealistic restrictions associated with this sect. My younger years were laden with frustration and disappointment. I became dissatisfied with my overall life situation. I felt trapped -- the significant choices that I had made for my life conflicted with my religious upbringing. I had a strong desire to reach my full potential. And I believed that if I was given the opportunity to do so that my life would be fulfilling and meaningful.

I wanted to sing in the school choir. I *could not.* I wanted to go to college. *That was severely discouraged.* I *could not* participate in community activities. I wanted to be a Girl Scout. I *could not.* I could go on and on.

When I reached adulthood, I was finally free to make different choices. I believe that the negative restrictions, personal frustrations, and experiences in my early years helped me to successfully overcome negative influences in my life. I was determined, even when I felt powerless to act, that no matter what, I would overcome negative forces and come out on top.

Because of the many frustrations I experienced growing up, I developed a particular vulnerability to managing negative experiences and overcoming obstacles. In other words, I have had my moments with negative issues. I've had my moments of spending too much time wallowing in self-pity when faced with difficult challenges. I am still struggling with this. But I have come a long way and continue to pray every day to overcome this challenge by adopting an optimistic approach to life's experiences.

I can't say with certainty that I've had more negative things happen to me in my life than the average person. But I can say, for sure, that I was deeply affected by them. However, I believed it was important for me to master the skill of shifting negative circumstances to positive outcomes. I learned that it was primarily an attitude change. I learned to switch gears and focus on problem solving, rather than let the negative experiences get me down. I call this approach *Negative Turns*. This approach has helped me to succeed in accomplishing many of my personal and professional goals. I have learned to do this throughout my entire life, and that is why I wrote this book.

This book is meant to be positive, hopeful, uplifting, and full of lessons on how to effectively soar through your daily life. This book can help you to deal with negative experiences in your life – at work, at home, with friends, family – any circumstance that is blocking your path to accomplishing your goals and dreams. The ultimate, challenge, however is to take action and – Make Your Dreams Come True.

Had lots of obstacles in your life?

Rejoice!

You have been chosen!

Your Future is Guaranteed for Success!

Chapter 1

BELIEVE YOU HAVE
CONTROL OVER YOUR LIFE

I was talking to my aunt on the phone one evening. She was telling me a story about a friend for whom she had a great deal of respect and admiration. For many years, this friend lived with a provocateur. Without recounting the entire scenario, the bottom line is that this provoking person was irresponsible, emotionally abusive, uncaring, and, to say the least, quite difficult. After listening to this story, out of my mouth came the words, "Well, it looks like your friend needs to give this individual a *ticket to Hell.*" My aunt and I both chuckled about my response and then agreed this was indeed a sober solution to the problem. The next day I thought about that conversation and decided that I should have added to that response: *"a **permanent** one-way ticket to Hell."* In other words, it should be a life sentence with no chance of parole.

My comeback to this story evolves from an attitude developed over years of frustration, heartache, and ultimately success, while managing numerous negative forces and situations that were placed before me. One of the major lessons I learned is that you must believe you have the power to direct your life.

This attitude is particularly important in situations where you may have encountered individuals in your personal and/or professional life who have caused you nothing but pain and heartache; individuals who have proven to be counterproductive to your purpose. These types of individuals can rob you of positive energy flow. You must learn to move on and search for those who want something positive for themselves and the people around them. I'm not saying that all your associations must be perfect specimens. There is no such creature of whom I'm aware. What I am saying is -- begin to search for individuals who have a caring heart and a positive purpose in their lives – individuals who are determined and focused on being their best. You will know who they are. Be patient --you will find them because they are looking for someone like you who share their aspirations. Circumstances will bring you together.

You can help the process by just believing you have the power to make your life what you want it to be. You must also believe you have the power to change your life, take control, and do whatever is necessary to make your life better.

Control Comes From Within

My grandmother taught me my first lesson in how to take control of your life. Gram, as we all called her, was the epitome of grace and charm. And if you had the opportunity to sit and talk to Gram, you would quickly notice that she would respond to most everything you said with the phrase:

"That is so nice," or sometimes the response would be: "Isn't that wonderful?" She always passed on constant reminders and powerful reinforcement to help keep your life experiences in the positive realm.

Gram was extremely lady-like, always had a smile to give and a kind word to say. She spent her later years as a single woman. I remembered that she did not particularly like the chore of taking out the garbage for the weekly collection. So, in all her glory, she turned a mundane chore into a positive experience. She carefully applied her make up, then got dressed. She usually chose one of her flowered shirtsleeve dresses -- "high heels and all." and put on her favorite hat. And of course, Gram would not be completely dressed without her white cotton gloves. She would then carefully prepare her garbage container.

Now, for her final act, she would proceed to take the garbage out *in style*. She lived on the second floor of an apartment complex and had to walk down the stairs. As she stepped out of her home, she'd notice that the doors of her neighbors would slightly open, allowing just enough space to take a peek. Wearing that gorgeous smile on her face, she was on her way! Everyone in the neighborhood would watch and wait to see what Gram, as we called her, would be wearing. She would wave and stop to talk to everyone she would encounter on the way. She literally lit up the neighborhood with her gracious attitude and positive conversations. As a young adult, I was in awe of her and wondered how she attained such awesome *spirit*.

Taking out the garbage was not just a mundane task for her. Gram looked forward to this weekly ritual. She believed it was up to her to make her life and everything in it a positive force. She took command of a situation she did not favor a great deal. She made it a positive experience not only for herself but also for her neighbors and others in the neighborhood.

I will always remember and share this story with friends and acquaintances. Gram affected my life in ways that she will never know. She helped me understand how important it was to believe that you have control over your life. And that you must act on this belief each and every day and know that you can turn your challenges into opportunities.

TURNS

Date: _____

Believe That You Have Control Over Your Life

Get started -- get your pen or pencil to begin your journey:

List at least 3 things you are going to do that will help strengthen your belief in yourself.

    1.

    2.

    3.

Identify people and/or resources that will help your carry out your actions.

        (to encourage and reinforce your accomplishments.)

    1.

    2.

    3.

Learn from others' experiences by looking beyond the obvious.

Begin your search for deeper meaning by asking questions to help you discover lessons learned.

Chapter 2

LEARN FROM OTHERS' EXPERIENCES

Little did I know that the personal experiences that were shared with me by some of my friends, family, and colleagues would provide me with continuous personal growth and wisdom. It took many years for me to appreciate the help and guidance I received from others. As a result, I have become a better listener and better able to distill a deeper meaning from others' experiences.

Here are a few of my experiences. Who knows; they may help you to learn something about yourself or help you to see things in a different way.

The Beauty Mark:

Experience # 1

NEGATIVE: When I was young, one of my favorite things to do was sit on a stool and watch my grandmother go about doing her daily housework. On this particular day, Gram had just finished her ironing and as she usually did, placed the iron on top of the refrigerator. It was now time for her to wash dishes. I decided to pull out my stool and put it next to the refrigerator so that I could be near her.

Like a typical two-year-old, I could not keep still on that stool. I began exploring the side of the refrigerator with my hands. I felt a cord, and I thought, "I wonder what this is?" Now at two years of age I did not know that at the other end of that chord was a very heavy object that could not possibly defy gravity.

I yanked, and my curiosity coaxed me to quickly look up to see what was happening. Within seconds the consequences occurred. The tip of the iron hit me right in the center of my forehead. I will leave out the unfavorable part of it, but the next thing I remember is terrible pain, being taken to the emergency room and getting my forehead stitched up. I remember the pain more than anything else.

I was told that my screaming might have been heard on the other side of the continent. This was not a very pleasant experience for a two-year-old, who had never experienced that much pain before. To add to the unpleasantness, I would bear a scar on my forehead permanently.

TURNS: Now, at the age of two, I had little knowledge of how vain women could be or how important looks were going to mean to me later in life. But, of course, Gram did. She immediately began to refer to that scar on my forehead as Euneata's Beauty Mark and pointed out how unique it was.

She repeatedly told me that everyone, far and near, would remember me because I had such an outstanding Beauty Mark right in the middle of my forehead. She told me that this mark was my special imprint, and that meant *"there would never be another me."*

Somewhere Over The Rainbow

Experience #2

NEGATIVE: My love affair with music began at about 8 years old. I began listening to music on the radio and would sing when no one was around. I loved singing. I used to dream of being an opera singer. I loved Gershwin's music. My favorite song at the time was <u>The Man I Love.</u> However, my music career was cut short. While I was in high school, I desperately wanted to sing in the school choir and play the cello. I did both for a very short period of time. I auditioned for the choir and was selected to sing soprano. My greatest dream at that time had come true.

Anyway, the Christmas holiday rolled around, and the High School Choir was practicing for a special program which would include singing holiday songs. Because of my religious restrictions, I was told that I had to sit out of the choir during the performance of these songs and could not participate in any way. I will never forget how humiliating this was for me. My music teacher would actually put a chair in the corner for me, and many of my schoolmates continuously teased me about it. I was devastated. I just could not bring myself to continue in this way. So, discouraged and humiliated, I quit the choir and quit the cello. I was very angry about this situation and at this stage of my life did not have the skills or support system to manage it very well. So, I decided

I would just give up on singing even though I knew I was blessed with a great voice.

TURNS: I still love singing. I kept my belief in my voice and resorted to using it in another form. I became a professional trainer and speaker for business and industry, and now, I use my voice to help and inspire others. My mission is: "Helping people succeed at work by overcoming barriers, building their strengths, and developing superior communication skills." Every time I speak to an audience or conduct a workshop, I am singing a song. If I can say the right words, it can be music to their ears. I wouldn't trade this kind of singing for anything else. I have a favorite T-shirt that reads: "The Sky's the Limit When Your Heart's In It." That sums up how I feel when I am in front of a group; this helps me to keep my voice in perfect pitch.

I found my purpose in life and that, my friend, is the ultimate gift for which I am very grateful.

WHAT A TURN!!!

Winter Blues

Experience #3

NEGATIVE: Growing up had its high moments, low moments, and just moments. This next experience is a funny one as I look back on it, but it helped me make a significant TURN.

I grew up in a small coal and steel town in Pennsylvania during the 40s and 50s. Most everyone on our street used coal to heat his or her homes. We had a potbelly coal stove that sat in the living room and a coal bin under our front porch.

I remember we had to take turns getting the coal bucket to retrieve coal from the coal bin to bring up to the house. When it got really cold, that potbelly stove did not keep the house very warm. I believe the insulation in our older, two-story woodframe house left much to be desired.

Anyway, it got so cold that when you spoke, you could actually see condensation coming from your breath. Some days it would be too cold to sit in the living room. It seemed that all the heat traveled to the second story in our home. My sisters and I shared the dishwashing chores and when it was my turn, I washed the dishes upstairs in the bathtub, because it was just unbearably cold in the kitchen.

I spent many a winter at home, too cold to sit still, no friends coming over, and washing dishes in the bathtub.

TURNS: I vowed then that being warm would be a priority for me. And there began my desire to travel to places in the world where it was warm all year round. That strong desire also affected my destiny and eventually led me to California where I spent over 16 years of my life. And later there was extensive travel to some of my favorite destinations: the Caribbean, Hawaii, Mexico, the Bahamas and Nevada.

That bit of suffering in the cold was the beginning of a passion to change my life experience. And, so it goes.

Career Challenge

Experience #4

NEGATIVE: At the age of 19, I moved to southern California to live with my dad. We lived in Pasadena, California. My first job was working for the Telephone Company. One of my goals was to eventually get my own apartment, move to Los Angeles to further my education and find a better job.

I interviewed and landed a job at one of the largest banks in California. My new position was Assistant Manager in the Trust Department. I reported to one of the most negative individuals I had ever met. It was my first day on the job. My new manager had a very disrespectful attitude toward me. In spite of it all, I somehow made it through my first half-day at work.

TURNS: Since no one invited me to lunch on my first day, I decided to go on my own. As I was finishing my coke and deli sandwich, a voice in my head said, "Do not return to that job; it is not for you." Well, I obeyed that voice, paid my check, and hurried my determined body to the employment agency that helped me to secure that position. I asked to speak to the manager of the agency and stated, "I cannot return to that position at the bank; please send me on another interview."

The very next day I was interviewing with a trade association. I was hired the same day and enjoyed a 9 year career with them. I was treated with respect and justly rewarded for hard work and high performance. I also received several promotions and significant career opportunities.

My new employer was instrumental and supportive in helping me continue my college education. As I look back on it, it was the best job I have ever had.

End of Experiences

TURNS

Date: _____

Learn From Others' Experiences

Identify at least two individuals you respect. Find a way to spend some time with them, perhaps over lunch or dinner. Tell them you are working hard at finding ways to manage negative forces and would like to know how they manage difficult situations and listen. Get ready for a learning experience. Do not probe, or pry; let them share what is comfortable for them.

Become a better listener. When others are sharing their experiences with you, tune in to the "greater meaning." This may be the tonic you need to raise your level of thinking and empower you to reach for the stars.

If you can arrange for a dinner or lunch conversation, **pick up the tab.** This may TURN out to be one of the best investment and personal development treatments you have ever had.

1.

2.

The truth hurts real good

Chapter 3

ENCOUNTER NEGATIVE EXPERIENCES AND TELL THE TRUTH

As a result of building a successful professional training, consulting and public speaking business, I daily take the time to think of ways I can thank all those who helped me along the way. I also reflect on the numerous challenges that played a vital role in bringing me to where I am today. I believe one can never forget from whence one came.

I remember an experience where I was trying to secure a training contract with a large corporation. To give you a little background information, when you are in the business of selling professional training services, you are actually selling yourself to the client. The client, whether they are aware of it or not, may make a decision based on your personal style, or how they perceive you may fit into their corporate culture. Being an African American Female has meant that in some cases, clients did not want to give me a chance. They would indicate that they just did not "feel comfortable bringing in someone of color." There is one case, in particular, that I will never forget. I was told by a manager, "You did not get a contract because upper management said, 'Do not bring any blacks in here.'"

Well, as indicated earlier, I was trying to close a large corporate account. I had been working very hard on this sale. If awarded, my assignment would involve facilitating a series of training workshops over a period of 6 months.

The training audience would be white male engineers, and my assignment would be to customize a communications program to improve interpersonal communication skills for the technical ranks. After several meetings with the decision-maker, I knew this assignment was a perfect one for me, but I also knew this was a high-risk decision for the corporate representative.

I was at a critical junction -- it was my final luncheon meeting with the decision-maker. I quickly sized up the situation. The challenge: I had to close the sale during this final meeting or possibly face the prospect of walking away without the business.

I had made my decision. After a pleasant lunch conversation, I took a deep breath and stated, "I know that this is an important training decision for your company, and I was wondering: Is the fact that I am an African American Female holding you back from making a commitment to me?" There was complete silence for about 20 seconds, but it seemed like five minutes to me. The representative responded, "Oh no, that is not it at all." But her non-verbal message spoke louder than her words. I knew I was accurate in my assumption.

I followed up by stating, "well I can assure you that if you or anyone else in your organization thinks that this may be a problem, you need not be concerned about it. I have a great deal of experience working with this type of population. If you grant me this opportunity to serve you, you will not regret it. I can personally guarantee that I will help you achieve your training goals and objectives." I left that luncheon meeting without an answer, but my intuition told me that the assignment was mine.

Four days later, I received a letter: "We are pleased to inform you that your firm has been selected to design and facilitate the Communication Skills Training Program for our company," I secured the assignment. I'm so glad I told the TRUTH!

This contract proved to be one of my firm's most successful and rewarding assignments, simply because I was willing to confront the situation and "tell it like it was!"

Based on my experiences in life and work, I recommend that whenever you are faced with a difficult decision, you must first analyze it thoroughly and decide on your best possible action. Consider timing and long-term ramifications of your decision.

In this instance, I knew I had nothing to lose. I also knew it was my last chance to act. There will be times when you will decide that walking away from a situation is the best decision at the time. However, when you know for sure that you cannot walk away, an ENCOUNTER may be in order. If you decide to ENCOUNTER, there are some very important principles to exercise:

- Be certain that you have clearly described your concern, request, etc.

- Ask the other person for their input; then listen (try to understand their point of view).

- Be ready to provide alternative solutions, options, ideas (be flexible).

- Talk in terms of benefits for the other person/organization.

- Do not walk away without asking for what you want. You must encourage action on the part of the other person.

TURNS

Date: _____

Encounter Negative Experiences and Tell the Truth

1. Identify an unresolved situation that still has possibilities.

   Describe the Situation:

2. Outline how you will resolve it by using the strategies listed below.

ENCOUNTER STRATEGIES

- Be certain that you have clearly described your concern, request, etc.

- Ask the other person for their input; then listen (try to understand their point of view).

- Be ready to provide alternative solutions, options, ideas (be flexible).

- Talk in terms of benefits for the other person/organization.

- Do not walk away without asking for what you want. You must encourage action on the part of the other person.

A FEW TIPS:

- These strategies do not necessarily have to be exercised in the exact order presented. They should, however, be incorporated into your interaction.

- To help you feel comfortable and confident with this approach, practice with someone you trust and respect. Do not hesitate; Get the Job Done!

Even if you do not currently have an issue to work through, you now have a strategy to help you in future situations.

Communicate More
and Watch Inspiration Soar

Chapter 4

DEVELOP YOUR COMMUNICATION SKILLS

Whether you are part of the professional community; private or public, an entrepreneur, a community activist, an artist, a homemaker, a student, or educator, you must acquire and demonstrate capable interpersonal skills. This accomplishment will help to ensure maximum effectiveness in your life and work.

I can safely say that I'm qualified to speak on this subject as I have spent years studying the impact of negative and positive communication interactions between individuals. Or it could be that I am rather biased on this topic, since I have spent much of my career training others to improve their interpersonal interactions in their life and at work.

Effective communication is the connecting link to high achievement and personal satisfaction. Without a well-rounded knowledge and practical application of it in its consummate form, you are fated for a life abundant with frustration and repeated failures.

My Biased Opinion:

Do you consider yourself a risk-taker? What would you consider a big risk?

Do you think investing a large portion of your hard-earned money in the stock market is a risk? Or how about letting your kids out of the nest, after being their major caretakers for several years? Or making a major career change? Or climbing Mt. Everest?

In my opinion, these are important, but not *substantial* risks.

Do you want to know what I believe *substantial* risks are? When you decide to ask yourself the question: How am I measuring up? When you must let go of an employee who is also a friend? When, after feeling shortchanged, you must ask for what you deserve? These, in my opinion, are *substantial* risks.

WHY? -- because you put **yourself on the line**. The final outcome lies in your hands. And this outcome is critically dependent on your ability to EFFECTIVELY COMMUNICATE.

Develop Relationships with Great Communicators

I attended a conference recently and for the first time in my entire career listened to a motivational speaker who spoke eloquently, *using no notes,* for approximately 30 minutes. You could hear a pin drop during the entire presentation. It was not just the technical expertise of speaking without notes, but the speaker's sincerity and honesty were evident.

This speaker not only communicated interesting ideas, but also linked those ideas to the audience. He talked about his experiences as a professional businessperson and shared some personal stories that demonstrated what it was like for him to struggle and how persistence rewarded him. He let the audience know, in his own way, that he understood the challenges they faced and that he valued their chosen professions.

I left that presentation with a new sense of pride in my own business and profession. I also left with an increased level of commitment to make a greater contribution to the clients and customers I serve by keeping pace with the changing times and making changes in my services to reflect those changes. Overall, I made a personal commitment to improve my level of service to clients, customers, and the community at large.

Later that afternoon, during the conference, almost everyone I encountered mentioned this outstanding presentation. The speaker's delivery and message, also, positively influenced them. A colleague relayed, "You know, I came here today thinking, well here goes another motivational speaker with a lot of fluff and not much to say, but instead I walked out of that room thinking what an outstanding, positive message."

Developing and mastering all aspects of communication skills can be a tremendous asset. In the case of this conference, I believe this speaker imprinted a lasting impression on most of those in attendance.

Making a commitment to develop your ability to relate to others can:

a. Help you turn people around in ways that you would never imagine.

28

b. Help you overcome challenges in your life and work that seem insurmountable.

If you are *confident* in your ability to reach others, you are less likely to give in to some of the challenges you face even when the road gets tough. You will always have hope. You will find yourself opening up new journeys on roads that were once dead-end destinations.

Effective Communicators Don't Have to be Great Orators

So, I suppose you now know why I believe it is important to have people in your life that you believe are great communicators. They need not be famous or accomplished speakers, just ordinary people you admire who have a gift for relating to others -- individuals who have had a positive impact on you because of the way they relate to you and others. They are everywhere -- in our families, at work, at school, at church, in associations, in the community, on vacations, volunteers, counselors. You know who they are, and if you don't think they exist, take another look. When you find them, develop a friendship for the purpose of sharing ideas and finding new ways of communicating.

Don't Underestimate Formal Training and Education

You can also benefit by incorporating some formalized training and education into your life. On-going education, training, and development are imperative if you want to continue to master the art of communication.

TURNS

Date: _____

FIRST LESSON IN BEING AN EFFECTIVE COMMUNICATOR

"KNOW THYSELF"

To get you started on the journey of self-discovery, take a few moments, grab your pen and respond to the following questions.

1. What are my greatest strengths as a communicator?

2. What are my greatest opportunities for improvement as a communicator?

3. Why is it important to improve my communication skills?

4. How can I best improve my communication skills?

5. What steps will I take to sharpen my ability to communicate with others in all types of circumstances?

A.

B.

C.

Develop Your Communication Skills
You Cannot Effectively Manage Your Life Without Them

If you can't feel it,
you are missing out
on the JOYS of intimacy

Chapter 5

EMBRACE YOUR FEELINGS

I was sitting with my partner one evening wallowing in my pain about a business disappointment. I remarked, "I sometimes wish I did not have a heart." He asked, "Why?" I replied, "Because I always seem to get the short end of the stick."

Well, I have rethought that discussion and after much deliberation, have changed my mind. I decided I no longer "wished I did not have a heart." If I "did not have a heart," I may not be sharing this moment with you in hopes of helping you learn through my life experience. If I "did not have a heart," I probably would not be able to give very much of myself when I go into a training session. If I "did not have a heart," perhaps I would not be able to pass through the mud to reach the mountaintop.

Having a heart may mean that I allow myself to feel the pain of life much more, but it also allows me to deal with my feelings, to acknowledge them and to let them take a natural course and provide me the opportunity to redirect them to greater places.

Find Ways to Express Feelings of Love, Compassion, and Caring

When appropriate, find ways to express feelings of love, compassion, and caring. Do not attempt to avoid these expressions. If you do, you will surely miss tremendous growth opportunities.

Recently, I learned that a long-time friend's son passed away at an early age -- mid 30s. I had not personally seen this family for many years and, initially had a hard time accepting his death.

I could picture their son very clearly in my mind. I remembered him as being very special, full of life. He was the adventurous type, and I remembered him being a very determined and sensitive person. I just could not miss the opportunity to let his mom and dad know how I felt.

What Crossed My Mind? Getting a sympathy card and sending it, calling to express my sympathy, sending flowers.

What Did I Actually Do? I got out my *very best* stationery and took the time to write a special note to his parents letting them know how sorry I was to hear of their son's death. I shared my thoughts about how I remembered him. After mailing the letter, I decided after the family had sufficient time to sort things out that I would follow up with a phone call.

I never had to make that phone call, because within a few days I got a call from his mom. We talked and shared thoughts of the past, present, and future. This was a special moment that I will always remember. I was glad I did not let this opportunity to *Embrace my Feelings* pass me by.

I am a better person for it. Why? This action deepened my ability to personally extend sympathy to others during a difficult time. Besides, It could have been *me* who experienced a great loss. It could have been *me* who needed expressions of caring to get through a difficult situation.

This experience helped me understand that sharing feelings and extending compassion to others is part of my purpose for being here. Merely living from day to day is not enough.

So, my friend, take advantage of opportunities to share love, compassion, and caring. Find ways that work for you. Your life will take a TURN for the better -- what more could you ask for?

DENIAL & ANGER

Now let's explore the flip side of love, compassion, and caring: Denial and Anger. Denial and mismanagement of anger can sometimes be our greatest enemies.

If we tend to go into denial, we are stuck in the moment, not allowing for change. If we leave room in our life for change, denials will not haunt us. Also Seek the Truth -- this is a commodity denial does not invest in.

Here are some stops and starts to help you along the way:

STOP	START
Lying to yourself	Telling yourself the truth
Lying to others	Telling others the truth
Defending people who don't deserve it	Pursuing those who are worth defending
"Should Have"	Say "I Will"
Pretending to be someone you're not	Being the best you possibly can be
Waiting for other to save you	Liberating yourself
Assaulting yourself	Forgiving yourself
Thinking you are weak	Believing you are strong

ANGER:

Learn to manage your anger; it may be one of the best gifts you can bestow upon yourself.

The first step in managing anger is to take inventory. Find out what triggers it and how you react to it. Answer the following questions:

ANGER INVENTORY

1. What types of situations make you especially angry?

2. What is your anger like and how long does it usually last? *(Does it go away quickly, last too long, occur frequently?)*

3. What are some of the verbal and non-verbal things you do when you get angry?
   (Get ill, refuse to speak, want to get away, become verbally or physically abusive, and want to hurt someone?)

4. Identify individuals with whom you have trouble dealing with when you are angry. *(Are they family members, co-workers, employer, employees, friends, etc?)*

Once you haven taken your anger inventory, you will want to identify areas for improvement.

SOME THINGS THAT CAUSE OR COMPLICATE ANGER

   a.   You may be fearful of losing a job or relationship.
   b.   You have been hurt.
   c.   You fear getting close to someone
   d.   You cannot accept being wrong.
   e.   You do not know how to calmly communicate when you are upset.
   f.   You believe it is not okay (normal) to be angry.

BEHAVIOR MODIFICATION STRATEGIES
To Help you Effectively Manage Anger

- Determine why you are angry. Sometimes it helps to write it down. Be specific. This will help you determine whether or not you need to take action or let it go. If you determine it is something you need to address, then move forward.

- Identify the outcome you are seeking. Is it equitable and doable? Think about alternative solutions. Your goal is a Win-Win situation, not a Win-Lose situation.

- Choose an appropriate time to discuss the situation.

- Remain calm; sometimes this may mean waiting for your feelings to cool down a bit. It will be to your benefit to be able to communicate with a sound mind.

- Avoid using blame, attacking, or bringing up unrelated grievances. Stick to the subject and work towards a Win-Win solution.

- Avoid statements such as "you make me angry" replace this with "I felt very upset when you said and or/did..." Then, begin to tell the person why his/her words or actions were upsetting. Focus on the impact the other person's action had on you. Stick to the subject and work towards a Win-Win solution.

- Try to listen and understand the other person's point of view. Allow yourself to be wrong some of the time.

- Set time limits for anger. If you cannot let go of anger or if you believe it is a big problem for you, seek professional counseling.

TURNS

Date: _____

Embrace Your Feelings

Learning to embrace your feelings means being able to manage positive as well as negative feelings. Mastering this expertise may take a little time and practice. Here are some ideas that may speed up the process:

- "Have a Heart" and take advantage of every opportunity to express feelings of love, compassion, and caring.

- Continually review the Behavior Modification Strategies found in this Chapter.

- Before you approach anyone or put these strategies to work, practice and get feedback from someone you can trust.

Keep counting your blessings
and you will have to hire a helper

Chapter 6

ASSURED EXPECTANCY AND
MENTAL PREPARATION

I was attending a business conference at a local college in Ohio. There were door prizes to be given away right after lunch. In order to qualify, each attendee was asked to drop his/her business card in a bowl at the registration desk. I met several interesting people that day, got caught up in stimulating conversations, and forgot to deposit my business card.

Knowing I would not be included in the drawing, I left the dining room early and decided to take a few moments to relax and have some private time before the next session started.

I was sitting alone in the auditorium browsing through my conference material when a woman approached me and asked, "Are you Euneata Payne?" I said, "Yes." She then said, "You have just won a door prize!" and handed me a beautifully decorated bag. I quickly replied, "But there must be some mistake, I did not drop my card in the bowl," and she said, "Well, it was your name they called. You do spell it E-U-N-E- A-T-A, right?" I said, "Yes that's right." Then she replied, "Well, I've got the right person, and this is yours." With a name as unique as mine, I knew the prize had to belong to me.

I opened the bag; there was a lovely fragrance of lilacs, one of my favorite flowers. The bag was filled with perfumed bath oils and numerous personal accessory items. This was one of the nicest gifts I have ever received. At the bottom of the bag was a card indicating the name of the sponsor who donated the gift. I immediately recognized the name as a business acquaintance that I had not seen in quite some time. She probably recognized my name on the registration list and decided to surprise me. What a surprise! I don't know why she decided to give me this gift, but I do know that I did not expect it; after all, I failed to drop my business card in the bowl. However, the most meaningful thing about this surprise is that it Made My Day!

This beautiful gift made up for the times when there was no Thank You.

Times When:

- I went out of my way to help others accomplish their business goals.

- I spent hours to write a 25-page training proposal, and the designated party decided he/she had no need for the training after all.

- I stayed up all night to do extra work on a program, and no one said, "We appreciate your effort."

- I gave more than I promised and never received any acknowledgment.

I could go on an on, but I think you get my drift.

No, my friend, things do not always come to you when you expect them. But don't be concerned. If you believe you give much more than you receive, it's okay; keep on doing it because wonderful things are being stored up for you, stored up and waiting for the right moment to descend upon you. And when your surprises arrive, you may think, "I did not deserve this." But think again, and change your attitude to one of **Assured Expectancy.**

Assured Expectancy is a quality that you deserve to possess.
It is the ability to acquire and maintain an overall attitude of enthusiasm and optimism.

Assured Expectancy can prevent you from getting discouraged. Remember that Life isn't always fair, but it can be sweetened if you possess.
Assured Expectancy.

Be Prepared for Expectancy of a "Different Kind"

I didn't expect to be dumped in the middle of the ocean, but let me tell you how I survived and what I learned.

I was vacationing with my partner in the Bahamas. We were just leisurely enjoying the beach, watching other people go out and enjoy water-sport activities -- parasailing, jet-skiing, banana boat excursions, etc.

I decided I would try my hand at something. I analyzed the risk factors and decided I did not want to parasail or jet-ski. I could just see myself being carried away, never to return again -- especially since I could not swim!

I made my decision. BANANA BOAT RIDING WOULD BE MY NEWFOUND ADVENTURE. I thought that the banana boat was something I could handle. It seemed simple enough. You just jump aboard an inflated creation in the shape of a banana, pulled by a speedboat. You are not alone; 3-4 other people are seated in front and back of you. I thought, "No problem, I can do this." After all, I had sat on the beach all day and watched banana boat adventurers successfully come and go. And every single person came back from his/her excursion with smiles, and a look of *thrill seeker's fulfillment* on their faces. Now, it was my turn!

I remembered the banana boat driver calling out, "Last Call For The Day!" The four of us put on our life jackets, hopped aboard, and we were off. I knew we were moving quite rapidly, because within a short time after take off, I looked over my shoulder and I could no longer see the shoreline. *It was at this moment that I got up enough nerve to mention to my group that I was a non-swimmer.*

Within a few seconds, we had completely flipped over and what I noticed before going under, is that the speedboat driver had not yet realized we were dumped. And the music from <u>Jaws</u>, the movie, rang in my ears as I descended into the water several feet down. Now you must understand, not being water-savvy, I had no idea that I was going to go under the water as I did. I thought that the life jacket would just keep me afloat when I hit the water. So I'm sure you can imagine how I felt when my body went under. Believe me, it seemed like I was going into an endless black hole. At this point I truly believed that I was going to die.

When I finally came up out of the ocean, I was petrified. I looked around for my associates; they were also coming up out of the water and frantically looking to see if everyone was accounted for. I believe they all decided, since I was the most petrified and the only non-swimmer, that I should be the first to get back into the boat. By this time, the speedboat was headed towards us, it seemed that it took forever and the music from <u>Jaws</u> was still drumming in my brain.

Our driver let down a steel ladder from the boat, and everyone was trying to move me towards the ladder. I was frightened and trembling so much that I had extreme difficulty getting on to the ladder. In the process, I hit my leg on the ladder so hard that it started bleeding.

Well, needless to say, we all managed to board the boat. After we were safely seated, the driver asked: Would you like to try again? It only took one look into my eyes, and the driver knew immediately that a verbal response was not in order. He immediately headed back to shore.

<u>Lessons Learned</u>

What did I learn from this experience? First of all, it is possible to get through a life-threatening situation and live to tell about it. Second, things don't always turn out the way we expect. Third, I may have been able to minimize the stress and get through the situation more easily if I had been a little more prepared. Fourth, it is important to learn how to manage life's unexpected experiences.

Much like a wind surfer who must manage a vessel and the elements in a way that guarantees a great sail, you, too, can master the art of *smooth sailing* in your life, even if things don't go exactly as planned.

The art of *smooth sailing* consists of many elements. However, I believe there is one strategy, when effectively applied, can help you get through some of your the most difficult situations.

That strategy is <u>MENTAL PREPARATION</u>.

I coasted for approximately 6 hours while sitting on the beach watching other banana boat riders come and go. Never once did I anticipate anything going wrong and, if it did, how I might manage it. I watched others return safely from their excursions and did not once think about asking those troublesome "WHAT IF?" questions:

- **WHAT IF?** the inflated boat would burst?

- **WHAT IF?** we were somehow disconnected from the speedboat?

- **WHAT IF?** the banana boat capsizes? etc.

As I look back on my excursion, I now believe that if I had developed a mental plan of how I would respond to this type of situation, I may have been able to minimize the stress or possibly have prevented the leg injury.

So, my friend, I encourage you to commit to the habit of developing the skill of Mental Preparation. It will help you lay a foundation that promotes *improved outcomes.*

Mental preparation can help, just in case you are faced with an **"Expectancy of a Different Kind."**

Preparation can ease the shock and may even help save your life or the life of someone else. It is worth it to take time for mental preparation. All it takes is a small investment of time.

Do not coast through life. Make every moment count, because things don't always turn out the way we expect.

<u>TURNS</u>

Date: _____

Positive Expectancy

A. You may experience an unexpected treasure when you don't believe you deserve it, and when it arrives:

Count your blessings:

1.

2.

3.

4.

5.

<u>Expectancy of a Different Kind</u>

B. None of us knows exactly what twists and turns life holds for us. The best-laid plans can sometimes take a turn for the worst or surprise us and totally exceed our expectations. Whatever our fate may be, keep in mind the following:

   1. Mentally prepare yourself when you are about to do something you have never done before by asking "What If?" Questions.

   2. Keep going the extra mile in everything you do. It's worth it.

Old ideas may belong in the
Recycle Bin instead of the
Trash Bin

Chapter 7

SHOULD YOUR JUNK ALWAYS BE
SOMEBODY ELSE'S JOY?

Some years ago, when I was living in Cincinnati, Ohio, my sister convinced me to have a garage sale. I had never had one, never thought about it, and never had the inclination to do so.

Well, I did it! I cannot remember exactly how much money was made, but I do recall experiencing difficulty pricing the items, feeling guilty about pricing things too high, and feeling worse about pricing things too low. After agonizing myself for days, I finally settled on prices I could accept. I had an old waterbed and believed no one would even look at. It sold for $65.00!

To make a long story short, my first garage sale was a success!

I had another experience approximately 10 years later. By then I'd moved to Columbus, Ohio. My neighbor was having a garage sale and asked me to have one too. She thought we could increase profits since we lived across the street from each other. Well, I was going out of town that weekend and could not participate. So, she volunteered to sell my stuff for me and asked me to bring my items to her garage. I remember feeling that I did not want to take advantage of a situation by asking her to do my selling for me, so I selected only one item -- an old vacuum cleaner.

I asked my partner to haul it out of the basement, dust it off, and deliver it across the street. I went over to thank my neighbor for including my old junk. I took a close look at the vacuum that I had not set eyes on for 5 years, and I thought that no one will buy this, it looked awful and was not very clean looking. That is why it was retired to the basement. So I got a polishing cloth and proceeded to clean and polish it. And still, I had my doubts. I thought, "If I don't want this thing, who would?"

Well, I returned from my weekend trip on Sunday night. Monday, Tuesday rolled around and I thought that surely if it had sold, my neighbor would have informed me by now. I thought to myself, "Guess I will be returning that vacuum to the basement." And decided I would go over the next day to pick it up.

Just as I was sitting down to catch up on my reading, the doorbell rang. It was my neighbor who stood there with a smile on her face, one arm extended towards me and in her hand was $15.00. She announced, "Congratulations, IT SOLD." I just laughed and laughed. I never would have believed in a million years that anyone would want it.

She went on to tell me that an older gentleman purchased it for his grandson who was starting college and had just moved into his first apartment and needed a vacuum cleaner. She told me how excited he was to find this vacuum and how he was trying to help his grandson get his life in order. He believed the purchase of this vacuum would help him get off to a good start.

WHAT ABOUT JUNK OF A DIFFERENT KIND?

The old vacuum cleaner I sold was a tangible item, but what about **old ideas**? Well, I recommend that you not get so set in your ways that you become afraid to return to old ideas and methods of the past. How many times have you said, "I've tried that before and it didn't work." And then someone comes along, takes what you've tried, sheds new light on it, and constructs a new breakthrough. So, transforming old ideas into something new may be in order for you.

Now, I did happened to do pretty well when my neighbor sold my old vacuum cleaner. Of course having a new one to replace it helped out. But when it comes to old ideas, you may not need to discard them too quickly because they may just need a makeover.

Don't allow self-doubt to take over to the point of inaction. Learn to protect and respect your old ideas, no matter how antiquated they might seem. Don't throw away **all** of your ideas. If you do, you may be turning the joy of your success over to someone else and *then what?*

TURNS

Date: _____

Should Your Junk Always Be Somebody Else's Joy?

Think about it; you may not want to throw away **all** of your antiquated ideas. They could turn out to be your joy if you save them and decide to add to them, rather than give them away.

Here are some strategies to help you preserve some of your junk:

- Write down all those junk ideas that have been collecting dust. You may even have some junk you tried, and, in your opinion, just did not work. Let's bring your junk back to life by putting it through a new life experience.

- Identify the junk that you believe is your top priority and get rid of the rest.

- Take out a piece of paper, draw a line down the middle, and write down the pluses and minuses about your priority junk.

- Identify similar ideas. Explore the possibility of combining your ideas with the ideas of others. You could find that together you possess all the properties necessary to win.

- Get more opinions about your ideas by putting together a team of diverse individuals to stretch your ideas to their fullest potential. If necessary, obtain professional help, support, and guidance to achieve this.

- Approach someone you trust who is in a completely different vocation than yourself or someone from a different culture. You may need to utilize your personal and/or professional network to find this person. You will want to get feedback about your ideas from this person.

Prepare some questions prior to your meeting and LISTEN. Make the most of this interaction.

- Now take another look at your junk. Determine what action you may want to take to give your junk a new life experience.

- <u>One more thing.</u> Identify any obstacles that may prevent you from accomplishing your goals. Determine ways to overcome them.

- Once you have had sufficient success with your priority junk, move on; you are now ready to repeat the process.

- <u>One more final note</u> -- let me know about your newly discovered **JOYS.**

When all else fails
GET MARRIED!

Chapter 8

MARRIAGE CONTRACT

There is not a single person on this earth who cannot in some way relate to the institution of marriage. We have all been touched by it in some way. Either you are married, never been married, divorced, thinking about it, never will marry, do not believe in it, unhappy in it, tried to help a few stay in it, helped others get out of it, and so forth.

As you know, there is a tradition associated with the bride that requires her to include *something old, something new, something borrowed, something blue.* To my knowledge, this tradition was founded in a rhyme that comes to us from old merry England, laced with superstition, magic, and good luck.

As I recall, the *something-old* tradition relates to an old garter from a happily married woman. If the garter came from a happily married woman, it could pass along her happiness to the new couple. The *something new* was anything at all, usually the wedding gown and symbolizes her new life as a married woman. *Something borrowed --* it was believed that the person who lends the borrowed item would receive a proposal within six months. *Something blue* symbolizes true love and fidelity.

HOW CAN YOU CONNECT THESE 4 TRADITIONS? TO YOUR LIFE WHEN FACED WITH OBSTACLES?

SOMETHING OLD

When you find yourself faced with a challenge, look back in your life and recall the many barriers you have overcome. You could not have possibly arrived where you are today without overcoming adversity. Give yourself credit for what you have done and what you have accomplished. It may seem like <u>ancient</u> history to you, but in reality, it is <u>significant</u> history that you must never forget.

It is also very helpful to share your personal stories of triumph with others. This can serve as reinforcement and a reminder of how capable and successful you really are.

SOMETHING NEW

Be determined to take new risks. This could come in the form of approaching a situation from a different angle. Don't always take the logical approach; use your creativity by experimenting. Do a little research to find out what has worked for others and modify it to fit your situation.

SOMETHING BORROWED

When faced with an obstacle, ask those you respect for their point of view. Inquire what they would do if they were faced with a similar challenge. You may find that you can borrow concepts from others that have successfully overcome similar challenges. You can eliminate the notion of trying to reinvent the wheel. This, my friend, could save you precious time and energy.

SOMETHING BLUE

If you are outdoors right now, or if your situation allows it, I want you to Look Up to the Sky! Yes, look up; look beyond the clouds. What color is the sky? Blue, of course. That *Something Blue* can serve as a beacon for you. According to the study of color therapy, colors can affect the center of the emotions, and the physical effects of the color blue are calming and relaxing. Its attributes are quiet strength, peace, and faith.

So, my friend, when the road gets rough, all you need to do is LOOK UP! LOOK UP to see that *Something Blue.* It is the association with that blue sky that will help you to continuously rise to the occasion.

Make a marriage contract with yourself. Be determined that whenever you encounter a difficult situation that you will incorporate:

- **Something Old**

- **Something New**

- **Something Borrowed**

- **Something Blue**

**This is one sure way to help you
TURN negative challenges around.**

TURNS

Date: _____

Getting Married

Make it a tradition in your life to apply the principles of Something Old, Something New, Something Borrowed and Something Blue.

When applied consistently and effectively, these guidelines will help you overcome barriers and bring you closer to your destination.

Grab your pen. Describe a difficult situation or challenge you would like to work on:

How can you begin to turn conditions around by applying?

1. SOMETHING OLD (Recall and list past successes.)

2. SOMETHING NEW (Look for a new approach, something untried.)

3. <u>SOMETHING BORROWED</u> (Whom could you approach to get help with your circumstances? Ask this person what he/she might do in your situation and/or has he/she encountered something similar. If so, how did he/she handle it? Listen earnestly.)

4. <u>SOMETHING BLUE</u> (Look up, at the *Blue* sky and shift your attitude from possible doubt to faith and conviction.)

Now I understand why music
conductors have so much fun

Chapter 9

DRIVING MUSIC

One of the challenges of being an entrepreneur is that you must do many things that you don't want to do. In my situation, one of the things on my Must Do list is travel. It can be draining at times. Some of my training assignments and/or speaking engagements require air travel. Some business is within the state, which allows me to drive. It is not so much the getting there, but it is the getting back home. Some of those drives home seem like an eternity.

I have discovered that what makes the difference is being able to manage my personal environment. So, I have taken great pains to select my very own driving music. Over the many years of travel, I have chosen only a select few. At this time in my life, they are Sarah Vaughn, Tony Bennett, and Johnny Mathis. They are my allies whose role it is to *bring me home.* The role they play has a tremendous impact on my energy and emotional state. While spending time with them, I experience the sensation of:

- Floating on a cloud

- Riding on a plane

- Conquering the world

- Effortlessly solving complex challenges

And when I pick up my car phone to let my partner know that either Tony, Sarah, or Johnny is bringing me home, he knows that I will not only arrive safe and sound, but in a magnificent state of mind.

Your Driving Music refers to the kind of environment you choose for yourself, your personal climate, friends, and associations.

I have applied this Driving Music concept to my entire life. I believe that I can create a sound environment for myself making enhanced choices, choices about with whom I spend my precious time while experiencing life's journey.

If you can get through life unscathed with a half a century under your belt, like I have, then you're ahead of the game. My diverse life experiences have taught me to place a higher value on myself, the choices I make, and the company I keep. This was a significant discovery and will help me as I enter the second half of my life.

I also decided to deepen the relationships that were in my life from the beginning of time. There is something special about connecting to those who knew you *"when."* -- those with whom you have shared unique experiences. There is something "special" about fellowshipping with individuals you cannot fool because they know the *"real you."* They love you unconditionally and are looking out for your best interest, not personal gain.

So, choose your Driving Music carefully. If you do, you'll discover new possibilities and opportunities. Remember you still have quite a way to go on your journey and; who knows, you just may be on the threshold of a major breakthrough. Suitable Driving Music can make a major difference in your life, more than you could possibly imagine!

Be discriminating; select your Driving Music carefully. It will impact your entire life in many ways.

Driving Music affects your energy, attitude,
and mental condition.

Superior Driving Music holds the key to your prosperity.

Answer the following questions.

Is your driving music:

- In Concert With Your Existing Goals?

- Positive?

- Consistent and Honest?

- Encouraging and Supportive?

- Steadfast and Focused?

Remember; you are on an almighty journey; therefore, do not hesitate to change the music as often as necessary.

Some transformations and/or elimination may be necessary, particularly if you find that your current music is destructive to your direction. Your choices could determine whether you will reach your full potential.

Take it from me; suitable Driving Music will bring you home to a magnificent rainbow of good health, happiness, and prosperity.

TURNS

Date: _____

Driving Music

To accomplish your life goals, you must carefully choose your driving music. Your driving music represents your personal environment, friends, partners, and associations.

Evaluate your life now by answering the following questions?

What do I like most about my current driving music?

What elements of my current driving music would I like to change?

What action steps must I take to better manage my driving music?

What support will I need to accomplish it? (Your support should consist of people + resources. You will need both to get the job done)

Continually work at improving your driving music. As you go about your busy life, stop to evaluate where you are; ask why and why not? Who knows; perhaps all you need in your life is a little variation in your driving music.

Seek the extraordinary in all that you do.

I often use this principle when going
out to dinner. I will ask the server,
"What is your **best choice** on the menu?

I'm rarely disappointed. As a matter of
fact,
this approach almost always guarantees
a delicious meal.

Chapter 10

SET HIGH STANDARDS
OF PERFORMANCE

It was a Monday morning -- a typical, administrative day at the office. I was executing my usual *Monday Program Research Grind.* The phone rang -- I answered and a mature-sounding voice on the other end asked: **"Can I speak to the gentleman who would be the owner of the company?"** I hesitated for just a few seconds and calmly replied: "I am the owner," and with a little chuckle in my voice, I added, "And I promise not to disappoint you, how can I help you?" Well, that got us both laughing, and the caller sincerely apologized for his opening statement.

In the past, this type of comment would have caused me to become very irritated, and I may have come back with a negative reply. But after a few years of mastering the use of my "built-in performance gauge," I am now able to effectively manage these challenging situations. My performance standards demand that *no matter how offended I may be by another person's remark, that I should think before I speak and avoid harsh rebuttals.*

My indicator also tells me that when all else fails, I should use my sense of humor to get me through it all. I've learned that we are all human, and can make mistakes. I've certainly had my share of blunders over the years.

When you set high performance standards in your life and work, you are sending a powerful message that you want to do your very best, not only for your own benefit, but also for the benefit of others. When you set superior performance standards, you make it clear that you *"stand for something."* And when you *"stand for something,"* others will stand up and take notice.

Future transformations in our society will require tomorrow's leaders to continuously work towards high achievement and superior performance. Quality of work and life will become a top priority. This will be accomplished, in part, by setting high performance standards.

Do you have unachieved goals? Go after them with high expectations and a set of well-defined performance standards. Do not rest until you have acquired and even succeeded your wildest dreams. You will gain respect from others, and more importantly, you will gain personal satisfaction and rewards that cannot replace all the money in the world.

There are numerous benefits for establishing high performance standards in every aspect of your life.

Here are a few worthy ones:

- Problems do not "get to you" as often -- You can minimize stress in your life and work.

- You have a built-in system that is constantly working to make sure you are performing at your very best.

- You will develop creative abilities and find new and different ways to get the job done. Your performance standards will not allow you to accept anything less than the BEST!

High Performance Tips:

1. Decide what your best will be, decide what you are willing to negotiate, and at what price.

2. Make sure that your standards are measurable. In other words, be satisfied that you can effectively evaluate your achievements. You must evaluate in a way that lets you know whether or not you've hit the target!

3. Is it within your scope of achievement? Do not set performance standards that are unachievable due to certain restrictions, policy, and procedures, physical/or mental limitations. This can be self-defeating.

4. You may also need to set appropriate time frames and deadlines.

Setting high performance standards in all aspects of your life can help you:

- Gain respect

- Build stronger families

- Save marriages

- Positively inspire others

- Overcome personal problems

- Beat depression

- Get that raise and/or promotion

- Effectively lead others

- Strengthen relationships and teams

- Promote a healthier workplace

- Give better direction to your children

- Help build quality products

- Protect the environment and save lives.

A life without high performance standards is a life predetermined for mediocrity, depression, and ordinary outcomes.

Make performance standards a priority, and then observe as your life takes a magnificent TURN.

Enjoy the thrill of it all -- you deserve it, my friend.

TURNS

Date: _____

Set High Standards of Performance

You must decide that you *"stand for something."* In order to *"stand for something,"* you must take a stand. Take a stand that your life will not be ordinary, that it will reflect the very best you are capable of giving.

In all things that you render, promise *the moon and deliver the moon and the stars!*

1. Describe something important you plan to do in the near future.

2. Identify any restrictions that you cannot control and decide that you will live with them, at least for the time being. (Keep in mind that circumstances can change in the future.)

3. In what ways can you make this duty your very best?

HOW WILL YOU KNOW THAT YOU HAVE REACHED YOUR PERFORMANCE STANDARDS?

4. How will I measure it? (Set a reachable standard that you can understand and feel comfortable with.)

5. What time frame do I need to set?

6. How will I reward myself for my outstanding achievements?

7. To whom can I teach these principles?

Only you can decide what your performance standards will be. Whatever you decide, be creative, be yourself, and, by all means, be <u>magnificent!</u>

FINALE

☺ Yes, You Can Turn Negative Circumstances Around:

☹Even when you encounter personalities who bring out the worst in you.

☹Even when you are disappointed with your outcomes.

☹Even when your children seem to be following the wrong path.

☹Even when your money is depleted.

☹Even when you feel you have no other possibilities, choices, etc.

☹Even when you did not get the promotion.

☹Even when you have given up on yourself or others.

☹Even when you are facing a disastrous personal challenge.

Just imagine if we could put a dose of belief, knowledge, truth, communication, feelings, creative spirit, a thriving environment, and high performance standards into a pill. And when those negative challenges sneak in, all we would need to do is visit our local pharmacy to purchase the *perfect potion*. Ahhhh…..life would be so much easier. **But Maybe Not!**

We would all achieve outstanding results in our lives. But that achievement would eventually result in increasing the cost of the pill, which would make it unaffordable for many. <u>Let's forget the pill idea -- which means that each and everyone of us must work hard to earn our</u>

<u>TURNS.</u> ☺

ABOUT THE AUTHOR

Euneata Payne, Professional Training Consultant received her MA from the McGregor School of Antioch University. Training adults since 1978, Euneata helps people and organizations leverage their interpersonal strengths, strategies, and skills to achieve results.

As a dedicated professional, Euneata has played a key role in human resource (HR) training and development for over 21 years. She started her HR career as Training Director for a division of Bristol Myers Corporation. She has earned her reputation as an excellent trainer who delivers incredible results for her clients as a workshop facilitator, consultant, and conference speaker. Euneata works with leaders and teams and provides customized training programs in the areas of interpersonal communications, leadership, team building, customer service, and performance management. She has been successful in helping adults make lasting behavior changes and take responsibility for their own attitude and successes.

Euneata began her HR career as training specialist for Bristol Myers Corporation in Southern California and advanced to training director for their consumer products subsidiary in Cincinnati, OH. She is a graduate of Antioch University where she earned a MA degree in Interpersonal Communications. Euneata eventually moved on to serve private and public organizations as an independent Human Resource Consultant. Her firm provided customized corporate training and development programs as well as public speaking services.

If you enjoyed reading **Negative Turns**, you may also enjoy Euneata's second book, **Piece A Cake.** This book can serve as a powerful tonic and inspire you to achieve your goals, and lift your spirits, especially during challenging times.

Euneata has also contributed to an essay in the book **Flowers are Forever** by Kathy Lamancusa.

I'd like to know how **Negative Turns** has helped you.
You can e-mail me at euneata@mac.com

The author will donate a portion of the net proceeds to charities which provide educational scholarships to underprivileged applicants.